GW01270717

'At Work' Series : Literacy at Work   ·   Photocopiable   ·   Published by Horizons (UK) Ltd

Literacy at Work

Published by Horizons (UK) Ltd

Junction 7 Business Park

Blackburn Road

Clayton - le - Moors

Accrington

BB5 5JW

Tel 01254 350035

Written by Sue Garnett

Illustrated by John Hutchinson

Printed by Marketing for Education

First published December 2003

"Tell me and I'll forget

show me and I may remember

But involve me and I will understand"

LITERACY AT WORK

CONTENTS

LITERACY AT WORK PROJECTS

CHAPTER 1

FOREWORD

From an early age children take an interest in what people do for a living.

Toddlers take the roles of doctor and nurse acting out the activities involved in doing the job. Once children attend school they take on a wider variety of roles including the teacher, the firefighter and other occupations known to them.

By the time children are leaving primary school they already have in their minds what they might want to be when they become an adult. However, they often have misconceptions and do not really understand what a job entails or what qualifications are needed.

Literacy at Work gives pupils an insight into occupations relating to literacy. It puts into place all the activities pupils do at school during literacy lessons and makes the lessons seem more relevant.

If children realise the relevance of lessons then they will be keen to learn.

If children can find out more about an occupation through a process of stimulating activities then it will give them a greater insight into an occupation and help them to decide if that occupation is for them and within their capabilities.

Literacy at Work can do all this.

CHAPTER 2

AIMS OF LITERACY AT WORK

School

- To give pupils an insight into the world of work

- To prepare pupils for the world of work

- To find relevance in what is taught

- To find creative ways of teaching

- To develop new skills

- To develop partners in the community

Pupils

- To learn about the world of work

- To develop new skills

- To find relevance in what they learn

- To develop confidence and self esteem

- To develop a positive outlook for the future

CHAPTER 3

INTRODUCTION

Literacy at Work is designed to help schools and teachers prepare for a project related to literacy in the adult world of work.

The project does not have to be undertaken rigidly.

Literacy at Work can be delivered as:

- A school project

- A class project

- To fit in with the National Curriculum

Literacy at Work can be delivered over:

- One day

- Several days

- A week

- Half term

Literacy at Work can be delivered to pupils of any age, from any size of school, with pupils of all abilities and from different types of cultures.

How to use the book:

The book is divided into two parts.

Chapters 1-5

The first part of the book is for staff. It gives a background to Literacy at Work and how literacy fits in with the world of work.

Projects 1-7

The second part of the book is for teachers to use with the pupils. There are seven photocopiable projects which include planning sheets for the staff and worksheets for the pupils.

Each project looks at a different occupation related to literacy at work

Within each project there is information on:

- Literacy links

- The occupation

- Company information

- Activities for pupils

- Extension activities for pupils

- Questionnaire about the occupation

What happens :

- The teacher chooses a project.

- The teacher decides how much time to give to the project i.e. one lesson per week.

- The teacher introduces the project and tells the pupils why they are doing it.

- The teacher reads the job information to the pupils or the pupils read it themselves.

- The teacher discusses various aspects of the job with the pupils through question and answer sessions and discussion.

- The teacher chooses an activity for the pupils to complete.

- The pupils may work alone, in pairs or as a group.

Extension activities:

Each project has extension activities. The activities can be used:

- With older/more able pupils

- As group work with a member of staff

- As a homework project

Questionnaire

- When the pupils have finished the project they fill in a questionnaire to find out whether the job suits them.

CHAPTER 4

EMPLOYMENT ACTIVITIES LINKED WITH LITERACY

Many activities undertaken by people in work include reading, writing, speaking and listening.

Listed below are some of the activities people do at work.

Reading

- Reports
- Factual information
- Letters
- Instructions

Writing

- Reports
- Adverts
- Leaflets
- Posters
- Instructions
- Letters
- Notes

Speaking and Listening

- Persuading the customer
- Understanding the customer
- Presenting information to the customer
- Diplomacy with the customer
- Sales pitch confidence
- Dealing with the difficult customer
- Public speaking
- Counselling

CHAPTER 5

PLANNING LITERACY AT WORK

Resourcing

The teacher may need to purchase resources to use during the class activities e.g. art equipment, computer software.

Converting the classroom

The teacher may wish to convert the classroom to look like a particular place of work e.g. Travel Agency – collages/pictures of foreign places, famous tourist sites.

Estate Agency – pictures of different types of homes, maps to show new housing developments.

Working with parents

Parents may wish to give their time in the classroom and help with activities.

Parents may wish to help the teacher set up the classroom for practical activities.

Parents may provide the school with names of contacts linked to their own occupation.

Working with business and the community

Prior to the event or on the first day, the pupils may visit a company or ask a representative to visit them at school to talk to them about the occupation they are studying.

The school may wish to find a business partner to support the school, not only during the project but as a permanent school link.

The business partner could provide time, resources or contribute financially.

The pupils could write about their business partner on the school web site.

MARKETING
FOR
EDUCATION
[creative marketing communications]

Graphic Designer

Graphic Designer

Teacher notes : Literacy Links

Reading

- Find information using contents and indices

- Research the topic being undertaken

- Use dictionaries to find useful words

- Choose and evaluate a range of texts for persuasiveness, clarity, quality of information

- Review what you know, what you need, what you can obtain and where you might find it

- Identify features of non fiction texts in print and IT which support the reader in gaining information efficiently

---

Writing

- Draw and make labels and captions

- Make notes

- Use technical language

- Write instructions

- Design adverts

- Select the appropriate style and form for your customer

- Use journalistic forms

- Use IT to bring to a published form

- Experiment with language and words

Speaking and Listening

- Discuss the product to be made

- Listen to other people's opinions about what the customer wants

- Give clear instructions making the product

Graphic Designer

All about graphic designers

What do graphic designers do?

- Draw and print charts, graphs and pictures

- Look at pictures and photos to plan work

- Sketch and draft ideas

- Lay out work using what space they have

- Paste and put together their final work

- Suggest improvements where needed

What skills and abilities do graphic designers have?

- How to use computer programs and software

- How to read and write

- How to use words effectively

- How to speak and listen

- Understanding of what the customer needs

- How to use colour and pictures effectively

- How to fit information into a limited space

- How to choose equipment

- How to judge and make decisions

- How to solve problems

- Coming up with lots of ideas

- How to manage their time

- How to work to a deadline

Graphic Designer

Company information

WHAT I FOUND OUT	Company name
	....
	Town
	....

FIND OUT

What do they do/make?

How do they do it?

How many people work there?

What equipment do they use?

Who do they sell to?

What do you need to be good at to work there?

What qualifications do you need?

Picture eg logo, building, office, product

Graphic Designer

Activity 1—New company logo

You have been asked to design the logo for a new company.

The company is called '**Start Right**'. It is a pre school nursery for children of 0 - 4.

Draw three designs for the logo. You could use the clip art programme on a computer to help you.

Think about -

- The colour and the font.

- How the design represents what the logo is advertising. Then discuss with another person the one you think would be most suitable.

- Make modifications if necessary to your design after considering other people's suggestions.

Graphic Designer

Activity 1—New company logo

Design 1

Design 2

Design 3

Graphic Designer

Activity 2 — Book cover

You have been asked to design the front cover for a cookery book called 'Super Snacks For Kids'.

You could use a computer programme to help you.

Look at the example below for a cook book called 'Meals Around the World' to give you ideas.

MEALS AROUND THE WORLD

By I M Greedy

THINK ABOUT

What the cover will look like to match the information inside it :

- Pictures e.g. buns, ice cream sundaes, omelettes, sandwiches

- Colour i.e. bright to attract youngsters

- Style of writing i.e. child friendly font

- Size of writing i.e. large for children

Graphic Designer

Activity 2 - Book cover

Super Snacks For Kids

Graphic Designer

Activity 3 — Web site design

You have been asked to design a web site for an up and coming band or artist.

Decide on the type of music they play eg pop, rap, heavy metal.

Design the first page of the web site.

Look at the example below to help you or look at web sites on the internet.

DJ Max

Home

Music

News

Tour clips

Pictures

THINK ABOUT

- Headings
  - Home
  - Music
  - Tour
  - News
  - Pictures
  - Extras
- Fonts
- Size of fonts
- Pictures/clip art/bullet points

Graphic Designer

Activity 3 — Web site design

Graphic Designer

TEACHER NOTES : EXTENSION ACTIVITIES

ADVERT

- Make a newspaper advert for a company that is having a sale e.g. furniture, clothes, electrical, musical instruments, jewellery.

- Look at some adverts in newspapers to give you ideas.

- Make a draft first. Include the name of the company, what they sell, what discount they are offering, pictures of what they are selling etc.

- Think about the style of writing and the size.

- Set out the information in different ways until you are happy.

POSTER

- Design a poster for a special event happening in your town e.g. circus, fun fair, fun run, holiday events at the local leisure centre.

- Make a draft first. Include the title, Where? Date? Time? Cost? Activities? Use adjectives to describe the event.

- Think about the style and size of writing.

- Set out the information in different ways until you are happy.

FOOD PACKET

- Design the wrapper for a new sweet.

- Think about the shape of the packet e.g. tube, box.

- Think about the name of the sweet. Use pictures and colour to match the name e.g. Sun sweets could be round and yellow.

- Think about the size of writing and the style.

- Draft out several designs and choose the best.

Graphic Designer

Is this job for me?

Do I like:	No	A little	Yes
Using the computer			
Using my imagination			
Choosing styles of writing and illustrations			
Laying things out			
Using different tools			
Drafting and changing ideas			

Is this job for me?	

Travel Agency

Travel Agency

Teacher notes : Literacy Links

Reading

- Find information using contents and indices

- Research the topic

- Use dictionaries to find useful words

- Choose a range of texts for persuasiveness, clarity, quality of information

- Collect and investigate use of persuasive devices

- Prepare for factual research by thinking about what you know, what you need, what you can get, what is available and where you might find it

- Identify features of non fiction texts in print and IT

Writing

- Make notes

- Select the appropriate style and form to suit a specific purpose and audience

- Use journalistic forms

- Use IT to bring to a published form

- Experiment with language and words

- Write letters

Speaking and Listening

- Discuss the product to be made

- Listen to other people's opinions

- Use persuasive devices

- Summarise information

Travel Agency

All about travel agents

What do travel agents do?

- Plan, describe, arrange and sell holidays

- Talk to the customer

- Work out the cost

- Book transportation and hotel reservations

- Provide the customer with travel information

- Collect the money

What skills and abilities do travel agents have?

- How to speak clearly and fluently

- How to listen to people

- How to help people

- How to read well and with understanding

- How to remember facts

- Patience

- Geography of the world

- How to persuade the customer to buy a holiday

- How to use a computer to find a holiday

- How to use a computer to work out the cost

Travel Agency

Company information

WHAT I FOUND OUT

Picture e.g. logo, building, office, products

Company name

....

Town

....

FIND OUT

What do they do?

How do they do it?

How many people work there?

What equipment do they use?

Who do they sell to?

What do you need to be good at to work there?

What qualifications do you need?

Travel Agency

Activity 1 – Persuasion

You have been asked to sell a holiday to a customer. Prepare a speech to give to the customer based on a photograph, postcard or picture from a magazine or travel brochure. Provide the customer with lots of factual information. Use the example below to help you.

THINK ABOUT

- Your style and body language.

- The information you will provide e.g. name of resort, facilities, weather.

- Positive comments and benefits. (Use interesting adjectives)

EXAMPLE

"Good morning…….. I believe you're looking for a beach holiday somewhere different. Well, I've got just the holiday for you.

This is Tahiwa. It's just five hours away and only half an hour's drive from the airport. You are guaranteed sunshine every day and there is always a cool breeze. It has everything you could possibly want. The apartments overlook the white sandy beach and there are two fabulous restaurants. During the day there are lots of water sports available and there is a variety of entertainment at night. It's just the holiday for you!"

Travel Agency

Activity 1 – Persuasion

Introductory script (welcome)

Manner (voice, style, actions)

Main script (reasons – facts, exaggerations, persuasive text)

Conclusion (summary of facts/information)

Travel Agency

Activity 2 - Letter

A customer is due to go on holiday in a week. However, you have received information that many of the guests have been taken ill with a viral infection and until the problem is rectified the travel company are providing alternative accommodation.

You have been asked to write to the customer and inform them of the changes to their holiday. Look at the example below to help you.

EXAMPLE: Cancellation letter

Horizons Sun Holidays
1 Sunnyside Road
Seabourne
Brightshire

21 December 2003

Mrs Y Hardy
25 Crabtree Lane
Dunninghan
Wellshire

Dear Madam

Holiday ref: 254034CA

I am sorry to inform you that we have had to cancel your holiday. The hotel is experiencing some problems with the air conditioning .

We would like to offer you another holiday at no extra cost. We have available the Hotel Royal which is just two minutes down the road from the one you had booked. It has the same facilities but is 4* and not 3*. The hotel is highly recommended and we hope that it will meet your approval.

Please contact us to confirm your new booking.

Yours sincerely

Tracy Gardiner

T Gardiner

THINK ABOUT

- Layout of the letter

- Introduction (why you are writing)

- Why the holiday has been cancelled

- Alternatives to the holiday

- Conclusion

Travel Agency

Activity 2 – Letter

Estate Agents Address

_____

_____

_____

_____

_____

Date _____

Name & customer address

_____

_____

_____

_____

_____

Dear

Yours sincerely

Name

Travel Agency

Activity 3 – Holiday itinerary

You have been asked to organise a three day holiday itinerary for a customer who wants to visit a foreign city.

Look at the example below to help you.

THINK ABOUT

- Which city you are going to choose e.g. Paris, Rome, Venice, Athens

- Where you are going to get the information from e.g. travel brochures, internet

- Places to see, things to do etc.

EXAMPLE: Cairo

Day 1: Pyramids

Day trip to Giza. Tour of one of the pyramids followed by a camel ride.

Day 2: Egyptian Museum, Papyrus factory

Morning visit to the Egyptian museum. See the treasures of Tutankhamun.

Afternoon visit to a papyrus factory. Have your name printed in hieroglyphics as a souvenir of the visit.

Day 3: River Nile trip

Full day trip down the Nile in a large cruiser with lunch included. Afternoon visit to local village to watch traditional crafts being made.

Travel Agency

Activity 3 – Holiday itinerary

Day 1	PLACES TO VISIT
	Cities
	Historical sights
	Beaches
	Leisure/amusement parks
	Mountains
	Caves
	Boat trips
	Museums
Day 2	**Day 3**

Travel Agency

Extension Activities

AROUND THE WORLD TRIP

- A couple wish to go on an around the world trip for one month during the Summer holidays.

- They wish to visit famous cities around the world.

- Set off from London and return to London, going east first e.g. London – Paris, Paris to Rome.

- Stay in each city for 3 nights. Think about how many cities you can fit in, in the time.
(Do not double back.)

- Further extension: Go on the internet and find airlines to take them to their destinations. Find the cost of the flights for two adults on single tickets.

PACKAGE HOLIDAY

- Find a 2 week package holiday for a family.

- The family has 2 adults, a teenage daughter and a ten year old son.

- They want to stay on an island in Europe.

- They want a hotel with a pool, by the sea, water sports, near the shops and with historical places to visit.

SKIING HOLIDAY

- Find a skiing holiday for a young couple who have never been skiing before.
(You will need holiday brochures or internet access to help you.)

- They want to stay in a hotel with less than 3 hrs transfer time and where there are plenty of nursery slopes and other activities. e.g. ice skating, bob sleigh.

- Provide them with information on some European ski resorts which will help them make a decision e.g. flight time, transfers, hotel, nursery slopes, activities.

Travel Agency

Is this job for me?

Do I like:	No	A little	Yes
Talking to people			
Reading and finding out information			
Using the computer			
Working with facts and figures			
Learning about other places			

Is this job for me ?	

Radio Station

Radio Station

Teacher notes : Literacy Links

Reading

- Locate information using contents and indices

- Use dictionaries to find useful words

- Prepare for factual research by thinking about what you know, what you need, what you can get and where you might find it

Writing

- Make notes

- Select the appropriate style and form for the listener

- Use journalistic forms

- Experiment with language and words

Speaking and Listening

- Listen to other people's opinions

- Put forward a balanced argument

- Summarise information

Radio Station

All about radio stations

What do radio presenters do?

- Announce music

- Announce adverts

- Read the news

- Read out requests

- Interview guests

- Read news flashes

- Ask questions

- Chat to people

- Discuss important topics

- Describe events

What skills and abilities does a radio presenter have?

- How to speak clearly and fluently

- How to listen

- How to read well and with understanding

- How to be understanding and empathetic

- How to be flexible in difficult situations

- Good memory

- Being original

- Coming up with good ideas

- How to manage time

Radio Station

Company information

WHAT I FOUND OUT

Name of radio station

....

Town

....

FIND OUT

What do they do?

How do they do it?

How many people work there?

What equipment do they use?

Who are their audience?

What do you need to be good at to work there?

What qualifications do you need?

Picture e.g. logo, building, office

Radio Station

Activity 1 - Interview

You have been asked to interview a local child who has done something very special.

Use a story from a local newspaper about a special child and imagine you are interviewing that person.

Work with a partner. You will both need to read the story carefully.

Perform your interview for the class.

THINK ABOUT

- Your introduction

- The questions you are going to ask

- How you are going to make the child feel relaxed

- How you are going to end the interview

Example

Introduction

"Good morning everybody. Welcome to Stars on the Radio, our weekly programme to celebrate local people in the community. Today we have a special young man with us.

Ben Garnett is only ten years old but last week he saved four puppies from certain death. Good morning Ben."

Questions

"How are you feeling?"

"How did it happen?"

"What did your family and friends say?"

Conclusion

"Well thank you Ben. Have you a story to tell? Give us a call on 01659 452391"

Radio Station

Activity 1 - Interview

Introduction (your name, name of show, what it is about)

[ ]

Information about the person being interviewed

[ ]

Questions

[ ]

Conclusion

[ ]

Radio Station

Activity 2 – Discussion

The topic of conversation on the weekly discussion programme is 'Computers and the effect they have on the children of today.'

You have been asked to prepare an opening statement to go out over the radio putting forward facts and information about the topic to which the general public can ring in and comment about.

Look at the example below to give you ideas.

THINK ABOUT

- What you are going to talk about e.g. mobile phones, smoking, crime

- How you are going to open the show

- What you are going to say to the listeners to encourage them to phone in e.g. facts, questions, controversial statements

Example:

"Good afternoon everyone. This is Ricky Moore on Radio Rock's weekly phone in programme.

Today's phone in is on the subject of diets. Recent surveys have shown that more and more children are in danger of becoming anorexic due to the media's perception of 'thin is best.'

Are diets good for you? Do we eat too much fast food? Do we need to slim as a nation? Are slim people healthier? Are some diets bad for us? Which diets work?

Call us on 01953 456329 with your views."

Radio Station

Activity 2 – Discussion

Introduction

Topic for discussion

Facts and information

Questions/Controversial statements

Telephone number

Radio Station

Activity 3 – Advertisement

You have been asked to prepare an advert to read out to listeners about a fund raising activity for a charity e.g. NSPCC, RSPCA, Cancer research

The advert should not take any longer than one minute to read out.

Look at the example below to help you.

EXAMPLE

"Good morning everyone. This is Sally Summers on 'What's Happening,' your weekly day time show where we tell you what's going on in our local area.

Well, we've got something special for you coming up soon. For the first time ever, we're having a sponsored fun run in aid of Walk to Live, the local charity for children with physical disabilities.

The event is taking place at Woodrow Playing Fields on Saturday 25th August. It's a five kilometre run and there are medals for all the finishers. The run will begin at 10am and the route will be sign posted so that we don't lose anyone in the woods! There will be a marquee selling refreshments and a raffle too with prizes donated by local companies.

Come along, it's going to be great. Everyone from the radio station will be there including our very own Johnny Jay who will be running in fancy dress.

Send off for your application or call in and see us."

THINK ABOUT

- Accurate information i.e. date, time, place, price

- Information about what is happening i.e. activities, stalls, games, food

- Choice of words to encourage the customer e.g. brilliant, the best day out, support a local child

- Time – only use the stated amount of time

Radio Station

Activity 3 – Advertisement

Opening line:

Information:
Where?
When?
Time?
Cost?

Activities/events (use adjectives, exaggerations, persuasive statements)

Radio Station

Extension Activities

CHILDREN'S NEWS TIME

- The radio station has a weekly news programme for children. Prepare the news report for the programme.

- Read a variety of newspapers and children's magazines to give you information.

- Prepare the news making it lively, exciting and what children will want to know about.

- Include national news and local news.

  Ideas: news about children, pop stars, actors, authors.

YOUR REQUESTS

- The radio station has a requests programme where people choose their favourite songs and say why.

- Choose up to five songs and tell the listener who has chosen them and why. You could ask your friends and family their favourite songs and why they like them.

  e.g. "And now we are going to play 'Angels' by Robbie Williams. This song is for Emma and Danny to celebrate their first wedding anniversary. Congratulations to you both."

NEWS FLASH

- DJs have to be ready to receive news flashes.

- Imagine you are a DJ and you have just received an important news flash.

- Read out the news flash to the listener.

- Give the listener accurate information e.g. what, where, when, who etc.

- Ideas: weather warning e.g. snow
  travel problems e.g. road works, accidents

Radio Station

Is this job for me?

Do I like:	No	A Little	Yes
Talking to people			
Reading and finding out information			
Reading aloud			
Interviewing people			
Working with other people			
Using my initiative and thinking on the spot			

Is this job for me?	

Library

Library

Teacher notes : Literacy Links

Reading

- Locate information using contents and indices
- Appraise a text quickly and effectively
- Secure skills of skimming and scanning
- Use dictionaries and glossaries
- Read and understand examples of official language
- Read and evaluate texts
- Locate books by classification

Writing

- Make notes and use simple abbreviations
- Write instructions
- Make records of information
- Make alphabetically ordered texts
- Write letters
- Select the appropriate style and form for the listener
- Use journalistic forms
- Experiment with language and words
- Write non-chronological reports and commentaries
- Summarise the contents of a text
- Collect information from a variety of sources and present it in a simple format
- Write a balanced argument
- Use IT to plan, revise and edit writing

Speaking and Listening

- Listen to other people's opinions
- Make a balanced argument
- Comment critically on the language, style and content of a text
- Summarise information

Library

All about libraries

What do librarians do?

- Organise collections of books, audio visual aids etc

- Review and evaluate materials to select and order

- Review and evaluate resources for the public

- Code, classify and catalogue resources

- Find information from resources

- Keep computer data bases for research information

- Manage programmes of activities for groups of people

- Assemble and arrange display materials

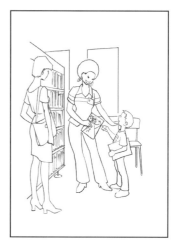

What skills and abilities does a librarian have?

- Knowledge of books and other resources

- Good memory

- How to speak clearly and fluently

- How to listen and help people

- How to read well and with understanding

- How to communicate in writing

- How to use different equipment

- How to arrange things according to rules

- How to resolve problems

- Ability to find information using a computer

- Well organised and tidy

- Ability to work in quiet surroundings

Library

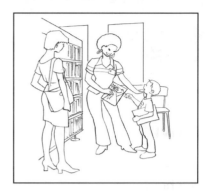

Information

WHAT I FOUND OUT

Town

....

FIND OUT

What do they do?

How do they do it?

How many people work there?

What equipment do they use?

Who are their customers?

What do you need to be good at to work there?

What qualifications do you need?

When can you start work there?

Picture e.g. logo, building, resources to use or on loan

Library

Activity 1 – Special Event

You have been asked to plan a children's event for the school holidays.

The one day event is to encourage children to use the library.

Plan the activities for one day. (You could design a poster if you wish.)

Look at the example below to give you ideas.

EXAMPLE

Monday 28th July

10 - 3pm

'Teddy Bears Picnic'

For children aged 4 - 7

- Book readings about teddy bears

- Teddy hunt

- Meet Barnaby Bear

- Fun size treats

- Teddy bear's quiz

- Free teddy puppet to take home!!

- Bring your bear along

THINK ABOUT

- The age group you want to attract

- What kind of event you want to plan e.g. magic and mystery, sport, characters in books

- The font and size of font for the information

- Activities the children can be involved in

- Illustrations you may use

Library

Activity 1 – Special Event

TITLE

Size?

Colour?

INFORMATION

What is it?

Date?

Who for?

Cost?

Activities?

ILLUSTRATION

What?

Size?

Style?

Library

Activity 2 – Book recommendations

You have been asked to recommend some novels for a new library member.

The new member likes fantasy, horror, humour and science fiction.

Recommend two novels and describe the novels to him/her. (You can choose the age of the person.) Make notes before you speak.

Extension: Work with a partner. Imagine they are the person wanting to borrow some novels. Ask them what they like to read and then recommend suitable books.

EXAMPLE:

Harry Potter and the Philosopher's Stone

By J K Rowling

Novel for a boy/girl aged 9-14

Genre: fantasy

The book

Harry's parents have died. He lives with his auntie and uncle but they do not like him. Harry finds out that he is a wizard and goes to Hogwarts School of Witchcraft. He learns how to become a wizard and how to play quidditch. He meets unusual characters and has an exciting adventure.

Good points

- Exciting

- Thrilling

THINK ABOUT

- The age of the child

- Their interests

- What each novel is about

Library

Activity 2 – Book recommendations

Book _____   Author _____

Suitable for girl/boy   Genre_____   Aged _____

Information	Good points

Book _____   Author _____

Suitable for girl/boy   Genre_____   Aged _____

Information	Good points

Library

Activity 3 - Project

A child has been asked to do a project for school.

They have been asked to go to the library and find information about their particular subject using books, videos, audio cassettes, CDs and web sites.

You have been asked to give them suggestions to help them with their project.

You may choose a project from the list below or choose your own.

Look at the example below to help you.

Extension - Work with a partner. Imagine they are the person doing the project. Tell them what they can use to help them with their project.

EXAMPLE

Project - 2ND WORLD WAR

Books

Carrie's War
Diary of Anne Frank
Who stole pink rabbit?
Children's war time diaries (fact)
Bombs and blackberries (play)

TV/Video

History channel
Goodnight Mr Tom

Web Sites

On this day.com
BBC News on line
Historyplace.com

THINK ABOUT

- Their chosen topic

  Examples:

  Historical periods

  Sport

  Countries

  Science

- Find out what they want to know

- The different types of information they could use

Library

Activity 3 – Project

Name of project _____

Books

TV/Video

Web sites

Newspapers/magazines

Library

Extension Activities

BOOK DISPLAY

- You have been asked to organise a display of children's novels on a theme.

- Make a list of books you could display for a particular theme. Write the name of the book and the author.

  e.g. magic stories, spooky stories, humorous stories.

VISITING AUTHOR

- A famous author is coming to the library.

- It could be someone who writes novels or it could be someone who has written an autobiography e.g. a sportsman or pop star.

- You wish to make a display of their work.

  e.g. JK Rowling – you could display all the Harry Potter books and also make a display of things from the book including a magic wand, cloak, glasses.

  e.g. A footballer: You could display their book with a signed football and football boots.

HOBBIES

- A young person would like to borrow some books on a particular hobby they have taken up.

- Find them books on their hobby e.g. skiing, canoeing, rock climbing, motor cross.

- Make a list of as many books as you can.

- Try to match the books to the age and reading ability of the person.

Library

Is this job for me?

Do I like:	No	A little	Yes
Books and reading			
Filing			
Using a computer			
Talking to people			
Helping people			
Finding out information			
Peace and quiet			
Keeping tidy			

Is this job for me?	

Hotel

Hotel

Teacher notes : Literacy Links

Reading

- Locate information using contents and indices

- Appraise a text quickly and effectively

- Secure skills of skimming and scanning

- Read and understand examples of official language

- Read and evaluate texts

- Choose a range of texts for persuasiveness, clarity, quality of information

Writing

- Make notes and use simple abbreviations

- Write instructions

- Make records of information

- Make alphabetically ordered texts

- Write letters

- Select the appropriate style and form for the listener

- Use journalistic forms

- Experiment with language and words

- Write non-chronological reports and commentaries

- Collect information from a variety of sources and present it in a simple format

- Use IT to plan, revise and edit writing

Speaking and Listening

- Listen to other people's opinions

- Use persuasive devices

- Comment critically on the language, style and content of a text

- Summarise information

Hotel

All about hoteliers

What do they do in a hotel?

- Greet, register and give rooms to guests

- Make reservations

- Keep records of rooms available

- Give and receives messages

- Answer questions about the hotel and its services

- Give information about hotel, local area to guests

- Provide facilities e.g. restaurant, entertainment, leisure

What skills and abilities do they have in a hotel?

- How to speak clearly and fluently

- How to listen and help people

- How to read well and with understanding

- How to communicate in writing

- How to solve maths problems

- How to resolve problems

- Ability to find information using a computer

- Record and maintain up to date information

- Organisational skills

Hotel

Information

WHAT I FOUND OUT

Name of hotel/chain

....

Town

....

Picture e.g. logo, building, facilities

FIND OUT

What do they do?

How do they do it?

How many people work there?

What equipment do they use?

Who are the customers?

What do you need to be good at to work there?

What qualifications do you need?

When can you start work there?

Hotel

Activity 1 – All about us

You have had an enquiry for a group booking e.g. scouts, guides, youth group, football club.

They are interested in booking a holiday in the area where your hotel is situated.

Speak to the chairperson of their club and persuade him/her to book your hotel.

You could go on the internet and find useful information from large hotel chains.

EXAMPLE: High Tide Hotel

Clients – Old Age pensioners

Introduction

Superior quality, caters for all needs, excellent staff, home comforts, guests come year after year.

Position

Overlooking sea, peaceful part of town, no traffic.

Rooms

All ensuite, tea/coffee making, trouser press, mini bar, sea views or garden views.

Facilities

Award winning restaurant, a la carte menu, residents bar, piano bar, evening entertainment, large dance floor, garden and patio with sun lounges, lunches and high teas available, special diets catered for.

Prices

Competitive, cheaper rates for bookings of over ten.

Three nights for the price of two out of season.

Conclusion

Luxury hotel with added extras.

THINK ABOUT

- The needs of the customers?
- Position of the hotel
- Rooms
- Facilities
- Restaurant
- Entertainment
- Price

LANGUAGE

- Adjectives
- Exaggerations

Hotel

Activity 1 – All about us (Group booking)

Name of hotel

Clientele

Introduction

Position of hotel

Rooms

Facilities

Prices

Conclusion

Hotel

Activity 2 – Complaint

You are the manager of the hotel and you have received a written complaint from a recent guest.

Write an apology letter to the person.

Choose one of these scenarios – quality of the food, cleanliness, rude/unhelpful staff, accident caused by safety problem.

Look at the example below to give you ideas.

EXAMPLE

High Tide Hotel
Beach Drive
Shingleton
Cliffshire

8th January 2004

Mr G Mason
Spiker Road
Prickleton
Deepshire

Dear Mr Mason

I am very sorry about the problem you had with disabled access and the fact that we had to move you to another room during your recent stay at the hotel

Unfortunately, we were having the annual health and safety check and due to a technical problem the lift was made out of order. Although we made every effort to help people with disabilities, this resulted in us having to change several people's rooms from upper floors to the ground floor.

On behalf of the management I would like to apologise for the inconvenience and would be most pleased if you would stay at the hotel free of charge some time in the future.

Yours sincerely

B White

Bernard White
Hotel Manager

THINK ABOUT

- What is the complaint?

- Why did it happen?

- What has been done about it?

- How are you going to satisfy your customer?

- The layout of your letter

- Using standard English

Hotel

Activity 2 - Complaint

Hotel Address

_____

_____

_____

_____

_____

Date _____

Name & guest address

_____

_____

_____

_____

_____

Dear

Yours sincerely

Name

Hotel

Activity 3 – Special Event

You have been asked to plan a special weekend event to increase the number of visitors to the hotel.

The hotel owners are looking for an unusual event which will be the first of its kind.

You could design a poster like the one below.

EXAMPLE

Easter Chick Weekend

GRANGE SIDE HOTEL

For all the family

April 1st – April 3rd

Special Easter menu

Easter egg hunt

Easter bonnet competitions

FREE Easter eggs for all guests

Cheap family rates

THINK ABOUT

- What is the event?

  e.g. murder mystery, 60's, hallowe'en.

- Where is it?

- When is it?

- Who is it for?

- What activities will there be?

- What is the price?

Hotel

Activity 3 – Special Event

Hotel

Event

Who it is for

Date

Picture

Activities

Prices

Hotel

Extension Activities

BEDROOM FACILITIES

- Your hotel has been refurbished.

- There are now a variety of bedrooms available.

- A person is interested in booking a room at the hotel.

- Tell them about all the types of rooms available.

- Learn the abbreviations for facilities.

    N.B. You could use holiday brochures or you could go on the internet and use a search engine to find information about hotels.

WHERE ARE WE?

- A family has just arrived at the hotel.

- They know very little about the area.

- Choose a local resort you know quite well.

- Show them a map of the locality pointing out useful information e.g. entertainment (cinema, ten pin bowling, museums etc.) shops, banks

    N.B. You could go on the internet and use a search engine to find a map.

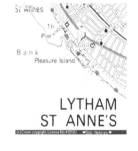

LYTHAM
ST ANNE'S

SPECIAL OCCASIONS

- The hotel is keen to develop that personal touch for guests to make their holiday more special.

- What special touches could you give guests in the hotel? e.g in the bedroom you could provide a fruit basket.

- What special touches could you give for people celebrating special occasions? e.g. champagne for a couple celebrating their wedding.

Hotel

Is this job for me?

Do I like:	No	A little	Yes
Talking to people			
Using the telephone			
Using a computer			
Working with people			
Organising events			
Filing, organising			
Organising other people			
Solving problems			

Is this job for me?	

Estate Agency

Estate Agency

Teacher notes : Literacy Links

Reading

- Find information using contents and indices

- Research the topic being undertaken

- Use dictionaries to find useful words

- Choose and evaluate a range of texts for persuasiveness, clarity, quality of information

- Review what you know, what you need, what you can get and where you might find it

- Identify features of non-fiction texts in print and IT which support the reader in gaining information efficiently

Writing

- Draw and make labels and captions

- Make notes

- Design adverts

- Select the appropriate style and form for your customer

- Use journalistic forms

- Use IT to bring to a published form

- Experiment with language and words

Speaking and Listening

- Discuss with a customer

- Listen to the customer's opinions

- Persuade the customer

- Give instructions for the location of a property

Estate Agency

All about estate agents

What do estate agents do?

- Display properties for the customer

- Sell and rent properties to customer

- Give people guided tours of properties for sale

- Find properties for the customer according to their needs

- Answer customer's questions

- Price properties

- Interview people who want to rent a property

- Keep records

- Oversee signing of contracts

What skills and abilities do estate agents have?

- How to speak clearly and fluently

- How to listen to people

- How to help people

- How to read well and with understanding

- How to persuade people

- How to come to agreements

- How to solve problems

- The ability to see details at close range

- Mathematical ability

- Geographical knowledge

- Ability to use the computer

Estate Agency

Company information

WHAT I FOUND OUT

Company name

....

Town

....

FIND OUT

What do they do?

How do they do it?

How many people work there?

What equipment do they use?

Who do they sell to?

What do you need to be good at to work there?

What qualifications do you need?

Picture e.g. logo, building

Estate Agency

Activity 1 – Property Information

You have been asked to write up the information for a property. It could be based on your own home or the home of a relative.

You could draw the property or use photos.

Look at the example below to give you ideas.

EXAMPLE

FOR SALE

29 Primrose Lane

Detached cottage on edge of town

Full gas central heating

Hardwood windows

Three bedrooms with fitted wardrobes

Bedroom 1 - 5m x 5m

Bedroom 2 - 4m x 3.5m

Bedroom 3 - 3m x 3m

One bathroom with 3 piece suite and fully tiled

Lounge with log fireplace

Dining room

Gardens with mature fruit trees and patio

Price on request

THINK ABOUT

Clear information:

- Address

- Type of property

Accommodation details:

- Heating

- Rooms/sizes

- Fittings

- Garden

- Extras

Estate Agency

Activity 1 - Advert

FOR SALE

Name

Address

Information

Price

Estate Agency

Activity 2 - Persuasion

You have priced a property. The people who are selling the property have estimated what it is worth. However, after careful consideration you think it is worth less.

You have been asked to talk to the customer and persuade them to accept a lower price by giving them all the necessary information and using persuasive. techniques. Look at the example below to help you. You could also look at properties advertised on a travel agency web site or in the newspaper.

THINK ABOUT

- Being polite

- Being positive

- Being persuasive

- Providing the customer with clear information

- Conclusion – repeating information, being positive etc

EXAMPLE

Address:

14 Crofters Lane, Grimmington

4 bedroom detached property

Details	Positive points	Negative points
Position	Rural, quiet	No local buses, trains etc
Kitchen	Large	In need of modernisation
Heating	Coal fires	No central heating
Windows	Hardwood	Some rotten windows
Gardens	Large, well stocked	Overgrown, broken paths

Estate Agency

Activity 2 – Persuasion

Property address

_____

_____

_____

_____

photo

Type of property_____

Details	Positive points	Negative points

 'At Work' Series : Literacy at Work · Photocopiable · Published by Horizons (UK) Ltd

Estate Agency

Activity 3 – Interview

You have been asked to find a rented property for a family. The family are from a different part of the country and do not know much about the area.

Interview the client (another pupil in your class.) Find out all you can about them and what they need. Assure them you can find a property just to suit them.

You could use information from local estate agents to help you.

Look at the example below to give you ideas.

EXAMPLE

CLIENT INFORMATION

PROPERTIES FOR RENT

Name(s): Jake Barnes, Kelly Hardy aged 19

Address: 25 Sandy Lane, Westpool

Tel no: 01263 497283

Occupation: Attending Birkdale College

Requirements:

Type of house: terraced

Bedrooms: two

Garden: no

Garage: no

Location: town, within 2 miles of college

Transport: On bus route for college

Other: near station

Time:

1 year

Price range:

up to £300 per month

THINK ABOUT

Introductions

- Hand shake

- Intro about you, the company etc

- General chat e.g. the weather, how long it took to get to the office etc.

The meeting

- Listen carefully to their requirements

- Assure them you can meet their needs. Be positive

Conclusions

- Sum up what has been said

- Assure them that you can find the place for them

Estate Agency

Activity 3 – Interview

Name

Address

Tel no

Other information e.g. family ages

Requirements

Time

Price range

 'At Work' Series : Literacy at Work · Photocopiable · Published by Horizons (UK) Ltd

Estate Agency

Extension Activities

HOW MUCH?

- You have been asked to value a range of properties.

- Find pictures of houses e.g. on clip art, magazines.

- Cut out the pictures.

- Put them on a large piece of paper.

- Put them in order of price.

- Ask a partner to put them in order.

- Do you agree? Why? Why not?

HOUSE MATCH

- You have been asked to find a house to suit a
  particular customer e.g. young couple, family,
  old age pensioner.

- Collect a variety of pictures of houses.

- Choose 3 houses to suit the customer.

- Discuss with a partner why you chose those
  particular houses.

PROPERTY ABROAD

- A customer has won the lottery and wishes to buy a
  property abroad.

- Find out what they want e.g. country, type/size of
  property, near mountains/sea.

- Go on the internet and find web sites of properties
  for sale abroad.

- Choose properties which match their requirements.

Estate Agency

Is this job for me?

Do I like:	No	A little	Yes
Helping people			
Persuading people			
Using a computer			
Keeping records			
Working in different places			
Looking at detail visually and on paper			
Working with facts and figures			
Solving problems			

Is this job for me?	

Newspaper Office

Newspaper Office

Teacher notes : Literacy Links

Reading

- Locate information using contents and indices

- Use dictionaries to find useful words

- Prepare for factual research by thinking about what you know, what you need, what you can get and where you might find it

- Choose a range of texts for persuasiveness, clarity and quality of information

Writing

- Make notes

- Make records of information

- Select the appropriate style and form for the reader

- Use journalistic forms

- Experiment with language and words

- Collect information from a variety of sources and present it in an appropriate format

- Use IT to plan, revise and edit writing

Speaking and Listening

- Listen to other people's opinions

- Use persuasive devices

- Summarise information

- Make a balanced argument

Newspaper Office

All about newspaper offices

What do reporters do?

- Gather information regarding stories through interview, observation and research

- Organise material

- Write stories for publication using the computer

- Conduct interviews face to face or on the telephone

What skills and abilities do reporters have?

- How to speak clearly and fluently

- Giving full attention to what people are saying

- How to ask appropriate questions

- How to record information or take accurate notes

- How to communicate effectively in writing

- How other people think and feel

- How to manage time

- Working to deadlines

- Reacting quickly to situations

- How to be flexible in difficult situations

Newspaper Office

Company information

WHAT I FOUND OUT

Picture e.g. logo, building

Name of newspaper

....

Town

....

FIND OUT

Who are their customers?

How many people work there?

What equipment do they use?

What do they write about?

How do they record this information?

What do you need to be good at to work there?

What qualifications do you need?

Newspaper Office

Activity 1 – Interview

You have been asked to go to a local school and interview some children about a special event that has happened.

Interview people from the school and write a report for the newspaper.

Look at the example below to help you.

EXAMPLE:

SUPER CAR WASH

Wareham School pupils in Brigham have been washing cars to raise money for their school.

On Friday 3rd October the pupils brought in buckets and sponges to take part in a Super Car Wash to raise money for benches in their school garden.

Throughout the day people from the local community brought their cars up to the school and had them washed and polished under the close supervision of Headteacher, Mary Worston.

"The pupils had a wonderful day and we raised enough money to pay for the benches," said Mrs Worston.

"I washed 7 cars," said Dylan McGuire. "I got soaking wet, but it was brilliant."

The school hope to repeat the event next year because it was so successful.

THINK ABOUT

The interview:

- The questions you are going to ask i.e. What?, Where?, When?, Who?

- How you are going to make notes

The report:

- Title, factual information, quotes, photos etc

- How you are going to make it appealing to the reader

Newspaper Office

Activity 1 - Interview

NOTES

Special event

Where?

When?

What?

Quotes

 'At Work' Series : Literacy at Work · Photocopiable · Published by Horizons (UK) Ltd

Newspaper Office

Activity 2 - Review

You have been asked to write a review on a film or video of your choice for the newspaper.

Look at the example below to help you.

EXAMPLE:

VIDEO RELEASES

'SPIDERMAN'

Rated: PG

Starring: Tobey Maguire, Kirsten Dunst, Willem Dafoe

Director: Sam Raimi

An action, adventure film for all the family.

Based on the legendary character of the Marvel comics, this is the story of Peter Parker, who lives with his aunt and uncle. A freak accident on a school trip gives him spider like abilities. Using his powers to fight crime on the streets of his city, he brings the person responsible for his uncle's death to justice.

Lots of exciting stunts and explosive action sequences will keep you on the edge of your seats throughout the entire film.

Critic rating: Great family viewing ****

THINK ABOUT

Name of the film

Information about:

• Rating

• Actors

• Director

• Critic rating

• Plot

Newspaper Office

Activity 2 – Review

Name of film

Rated _____

Starring

Director

Plot

Critic rating

 'At Work' Series : Literacy at Work · Photocopiable · Published by Horizons (UK) Ltd

Newspaper Office

Activity 3 – Weekly column

You have been asked to write the weekly column about a hobby or activity which interests you.

You could be an expert in gardening, football, cooking, pets etc.

Write your weekly report with handy tips for the reader.

Look at the example below to help you.

EXAMPLE:

GARY'S GOLF

Over the last few months we've looked at improving our shots. This week I thought we could take a look at beginners. Maybe you're thinking of taking up golf and don't know where to start.

Beginner's guide to golf

1.   Approach a local club and find out about lessons. Start your lessons. They may be expensive but they will be worth every penny.

2.   Go along to your nearest driving range and have a go. (They can loan you clubs)

3.   If you like it, think about buying a starter set of clubs.

4.   Make sure you get advice on the clubs you need.

5.   Buy some golf shoes. Comfort is more important than style!

6.   Practice!!

THINK ABOUT

- What hobby or activity you are interested in and know a lot about

- Title

- Information

- Instructions

Newspaper Office

Activity 3 – Weekly column

Title

Information

Picture

Picture

'At Work' Series : Literacy at Work · Photocopiable · Published by Horizons (UK) Ltd

Newspaper Office

Extension Activities

PICTURES

- Work with a partner to write a newspaper report based on a picture/photo.

- Cut out some pictures from magazines.

- You and your partner need to agree on one picture.

- Write your own reports. Are they similar?

HEADLINE

- Work with a partner to write newspaper headlines using stories from newspapers.

- Cut out stories without headlines.

- Give the stories to your partner.

- Are their headlines the same as the ones in the newspaper?

NEWS

- Write a news report for children.

- First of all watch the news on television.

- Take notes of a story which would interest children.

- Write up your information as a news report.

- Use words children will understand.

FUN PAGE

- Write a 'fun page' for children.

- You could include: children with birthdays, quizzes, competition, colouring, book/film review etc.

WEATHER REPORT

- Watch the weather report on the television. Make notes of the words they use.

- Write your own weather report using maps with symbols.

Newspaper Office

Is this job for me?

Do I like:	No	A Little	Yes
Talking to people			
Listening			
Taking notes			
Writing			
Working to deadlines			
Using the computer			
Travelling			
Investigating			

Is this job for me?	

Literacy at Work

Sue Garnett

Projects:

Graphic Design Studio
Learn how to design a company logo, a front cover for a book and a children's game

Travel Agency
Learn how to write a letter to a customer, sell a holiday and organize a holiday itinerary

Radio Station
Learn how to interview, lead a discussion programme and advertise a special event

Library
Learn how to organize a special event, review books and help someone find information for a project

Hotel
Learn how to persuade customers to come to the hotel, write an apology letter and plan a special event

Estate Agency
Learn how to design an advert for a property, interview a client and persuade a customer to buy a house

Newspaper Office
Learn how to interview, write a review and write a specialist column

ISBN 0-9543687-1-1

9 780954 368715

HORIZONS
(UK) LTD
Published by
HORIZONS (UK) LTD